Language Builders

Austin and Alex Learn about
ADJECTIVES

by Darice Bailer
illustrated by Patrick Girouard

Content Consultant
Roxanne Owens
Associate Professor, Elementary Reading
DePaul University

NORWOOD HOUSE PRESS
CHICAGO, ILLINOIS

Norwood House Press
P.O. Box 316598
Chicago, Illinois 60631
For information regarding Norwood House Press, please visit
our website at:
www.norwoodhousepress.com or call 866-565-2900.

Editor: Melissa York
Designer: Jake Nordby
Project Management: Red Line Editorial

Library of Congress Cataloging-in-Publication Data
Bailer, Darice, author.
  Austin and Alex learn about adjectives / By Darice Bailer ;
Illustrated by Patrick Girouard.
      p. cm. -- (Language Builders)
  Audience: Ages 7-10
  Includes bibliographical references.
  Summary: "Austin and Alex learn about adjectives while on a
camping trip.
Concepts include: basic definition and usage of adjectives;
comparative; superlative and predicate adjectives; placement
in the sentence; and comma use. Activities in the back help
reinforce text concepts. Includes glossary and additional
resources"-- Provided by publisher.
  ISBN 978-1-59953-668-2 (library edition : alk. paper) -- ISBN
978-1-60357-728-1 (ebook)
  1. English language--Adjective--Juvenile literature. 2. English
language--Parts of speech--Juvenile literature. 3. Camping--
Juvenile literature. I. Girouard, Patrick, illustrator. II. Title.
  PE1241.B35 2015
  428.1--dc22
                              2014030326

Manufactured in the United States of America in North
Mankato, Minnesota.
262N—122014

Words in **black bold** are defined in the glossary.

Word Pictures

I learned something fun in school today! Our teacher, Mrs. Freeman, taught us about **adjectives**. She said that adjectives are like a box of crayons. Adjectives are words that color in **details**. They paint a picture for our readers.

I drew a picture of my cat, Buster. I colored Buster's green eyes and his orange fur. I also drew his long, bushy tail. Mrs. Freeman held up the picture I drew. "Green, orange, long, and bushy are all adjectives," Mrs. Freeman said. "Adjectives describe nouns. A noun is a person, place, or thing. Cat is a noun. Tail is a noun, too."

On Monday, Austin and I are going to be writing buddies. We have to write descriptions of a noun using adjectives. The class has to guess what our noun is using our adjectives as clues. She calls this "painting a word picture." Austin and I are going camping this weekend. Maybe we'll get some ideas on our trip!

By Alex, age 9

"Austin! Alex! Time to pack the car," Austin's father, Mr. Lawson, called. Alex and Austin were in Austin's room. Alex was helping Austin finish packing his stuff for the camping trip.

"Just a minute," Austin answered. "I'm looking for some games for us to play while we're camping."

"What a brilliant, fantastic idea!" Alex said.

Austin smiled. "Way to go, Alex! Mrs. Freeman told us good writers use lots of **descriptive** words."

"Right!" Alex said. "*Brilliant* and *fantastic* say that your idea is great!"

Alex zipped the backpack he was packing and smiled. "I'm so glad we're going to be writing buddies next week. Mrs. Freeman always likes to read your stories to the class."

Then Alex's face turned sad. "I wish I could write better. Writing is scary, especially when I'm staring at those blue lines on blank white paper. I never know where to start. Mrs. Freeman wants us to use ten adjectives in our writing projects next week. I'm doomed!"

Austin laughed. "Hold on, Alex! You just used a bunch of adjectives. Like *blue* lines and *blank white* paper. And you said writing is *scary*. Adjectives tell how you feel. Like *scared*. Or *excited*! Adjectives also tell how many. Like *ten* adjectives!"

"Maybe coming up with ten adjectives isn't that hard, Austin!"

"Just think of your brain as a box of crayons. Pull out the words that draw pictures!"

"Thanks, Austin. Now let's go camping!"

"And I'll bring a *small* notebook and a *black* pen so we can make a list of adjectives!" Austin exclaimed as they stood up, grabbed the bags, and left the room.

Mr. Lawson was glad to see Alex and Austin. He gave the two children a job. "Can you pack the food for s'mores in Austin's big green backpack?"

"Sure!" Alex said. "You just used two adjectives!"

"Right," Mr. Lawson said. "*Big* and *green* describe the backpack."

8

"But suppose I had two more backpacks, red and purple," continued Mr. Lawson. "If I didn't tell you to stuff them in 'the red backpack' or 'the purple backpack,' you wouldn't know which one I meant!"

"Adjectives usually go before the noun in a sentence," offered Austin.

"Most of the time," Mr. Lawson agreed.

"They go in order, too. You use size before color in a sentence. Like big green backpacks."

Alex made a note in the notebook:

Adjectives go in order. Size, Age, Shape, Color.

"S'mores are delicious," said Alex.

"*Delicious* is an adjective, too," said Austin. "A **predicate adjective** comes later in the sentence. It follows a noun and a **linking verb**."

"Right," said Alex. "I remember linking verbs. They are forms of *to be*, like *is*, *was*, or *are*."

"Don't forget linking verbs like *seems*, *tastes*, and *looks*," added Mr. Lawson.

The two children stuffed the box of graham crackers and the bag of marshmallows into the backpack.

"We can fit a lot in your backpack!" said Alex.

"Yes," said Austin. "It's larger than the one I use for school."

Alex paused. "I think *larger* is an adjective, too."

"Good job!" Mr. Lawson said. "Words like *smaller* and *larger* are **comparative adjectives**. They compare two people or things."

"Like you're taller than my dad and my dad's shorter than you," replied Alex.

"Yes! You can add *–er* to many adjectives to make comparative adjectives. You can put *–er* at the end of *small* to make *smaller* and *–er* to the end of *fast* to make *faster*," said Mr. Lawson.

"Or if you have more than two things, you can add –*est* to show which one is the smallest or fastest of all," said Austin. "That's a **superlative adjective**."

"Right!" Alex said. "I'll pack the tin cups and bowls in the bigger backpack with the ingredients for s'mores. I'm starting to like using adjectives!"

Alex made another note in the notebook:

Remember what Mrs. Freeman told us: If you have a short word that ends in a consonant, double the consonant before you add –er or –est. Like big, bigger, biggest. Hot, hotter, hottest.

In the car, Mr. Lawson asked Alex if he'd ever gone camping before. Alex shook his head.

"Tell him what it's like out in the woods, Austin," invited Mr. Lawson.

"Use the best adjectives you can!" Alex teased.

"Hmm," Austin said. "Mrs. Freeman said that adjectives tell how something looks, sounds, feels, smells, and tastes. Out in the woods, you see tall trees all around you. You smell the fresh air and hear the crunchy sound leaves make when you walk on them. You feel scratchy bushes brush by as you walk down a narrow path. You roast a sweet marshmallow on a long stick over a hot fire and then taste your yummy dessert."

"Can you describe how you feel about camping, Alex?" asked Mr. Lawson. "Paint a word picture for us."

"Let me see," said Alex. "I am happy we're going on this awesome, fun trip. I hope we see animals, like a furry, cuddly raccoon or a cute baby deer. I hope we don't see a humongous bear! Adjectives do sing and make words more exciting!"

Alex wrote down in the notebook:

I hope we see a furry, cuddly raccoon or a cute baby deer. I hope we don't see a humongous bear!

"Huh," Alex said. "Why is there a comma between *furry* and *cuddly* but not *cute* and *baby*?"

"You add a comma only if you can say 'and' between the adjectives and the meaning stays the same," explained Mr. Lawson. "You can say *furry and cuddly raccoon* but *cute and baby deer* is not exactly right."

That night, the two kids found sticks to toast marshmallows on around the campfire. The wood crackled and yellow flames shot up toward the dark night sky as they toasted their treat. "My marshmallow's getting brown," Alex said.

"Mine's browner!" Austin said. "I used a comparative adjective!"

Alex laughed. "I'm going to make the gooiest, yummiest s'more ever!"

Suddenly Alex froze. "What's that smell? Something smells really stinky."

Austin turned on his blue flashlight. The bright light shone on a little black creature with a white stripe down its back.

"Yikes! A skunk!" Austin said.

"Yeah, a smelly, stinky, black and white skunk!" Alex yelled.

"And this skunk may be the stinkiest one yet," Austin said. "Run!"

Everyone dove into the tent and Alex hugged his knees. "This is the exciting-est adventure I've ever had!"

Mr. Lawson laughed. "We add the words *more* and *most* to long adjectives when we want to compare things. You would say that this camping trip is more exciting than other trips. Or it's the most exciting one you've been on."

"*Good*, *better*, and *best* compare things, too," continued Mr. Lawson. "When you compare two vacations, you could say one was very good, but another was better."

"Or bad, worse, worst!" Austin added.

"Camping isn't just good or better than other vacations," said Alex. "Camping is the best!"

Alex snuggled into his sleeping bag. As he tried to fall asleep, he kept thinking of more adjectives. Maybe it would be a sunny day tomorrow, or a sunnier day than yesterday. Or maybe it would be the sunniest day of the week! He took a word that ended in *y* and added *–ier* or *–iest* to compare. Like fuzzy, fuzzier, and fuzziest. Or sleepy, sleepier, sleepiest . . .

On Monday, Alex and Austin pushed their desks together. "Got any ideas for what we can describe?" Austin asked.

Alex smiled. "Camping, of course!"

Guess Where We Went This Weekend?
by Alex and Austin

1. We walked under <u>tall</u> trees.
2. But we tried to avoid <u>scratchy green</u> bushes.
3. The <u>sweet</u> smell of <u>sharp</u> pine needles filled our noses.
4. We heard the crunch of <u>reddish</u> brown pinecones.
5. We tasted <u>gooey</u>, <u>yummy</u> s'mores.
6. We saw <u>bright</u> <u>white</u> stars in the <u>dark</u> <u>blue</u> sky.
7. We snuggled into <u>warm</u>, <u>cozy</u> sleeping bags.
8. We smelled the <u>stinkiest</u> skunk ever!
9. We heard <u>brown</u> owls with <u>yellow</u> eyes hooting in the night.
10. We woke up to see an <u>orange</u> sunrise in a <u>pink</u> sky.

Mrs. Freeman clapped her hands after Alex finished reading. "Great job!" she said. "Can anyone guess where Alex and Austin went?"

All hands shot in the air.

Alex and Austin had painted such a good word picture that everyone knew!

Know Your Adjectives

Adjectives make writing colorful and exciting. A sentence doesn't need to have adjectives, but they help describe a scene and make a story come to life. They describe nouns so you can tell whether to take the red backpack or the blue one, or say which dessert is the sweetest.

In a sentence, adjectives often come before a noun: the *cool* breeze tickled your nose, or the *juiciest* berries are ripe in June. Adjectives can also come after a noun. A linking verb connects the two: his dad is *taller* than hers, and the stars are *big* and *bright*.

Find the adjectives in the following sentences. Some sentences have more than one adjective. Do they come before the noun? Or are they predicate adjectives that follow a linking verb? Can you find the comparative adjectives and the superlative adjectives?

Pack the tin cups and bowls in the bigger backpack.

The green woods are full of tall trees and twisty paths.

Maybe tomorrow will be sunnier than today.

My hands are sticky from eating those delicious s'mores.

Camping is the best vacation.

Writing Activity

Get together with a friend and play a riddle game. Call it "Who am I?" Think of someone you both know. Don't say who it is out loud. Write down five adjectives to describe the secret person. Meanwhile, your friend should do the same. When you are both done writing, take turns reading one adjective at a time. Try to guess the secret person from as few adjectives as possible.

Write a story about a place you visited. When you are done, circle all the adjectives you used. Can you replace the adjectives with others that make your writing more colorful? Try adding adjectives to sentences that had none.

Glossary

adjectives: words that describe a noun or pronoun.

comparative adjectives: adjectives that compare two things.

descriptive: creating a word picture of something.

details: words that give information about something.

linking verb: a verb, or action word, that connects a noun to the adjective that describes it.

predicate adjective: an adjective that comes after a linking verb and refers back to the subject of the verb.

superlative adjective: an adjective that describes the noun that is the most or best, like the *biggest* dog or the *cutest* teddy bear.

For More Information

Books

Fisher, Doris. *Bowling Alley Adjectives*. Pleasantville, NY: Gareth Stevens, 2008.

Reeg, Cynthia. *Hamster Holidays: Noun and Adjective Adventures*. Saint Louis, MO: Guardian Angel Publishing, 2009.

Riggs, Kate. *Grammar Basics: Adjectives*. Mankato, MN: Creative, 2013.

Websites

Adjectives Interactive Movie
http://www.kidsknowit.com/flash/animations/adjective.swf
Learn more about adjectives from this interactive movie.

Turtle Diary
http://www.turtlediary.com/grade-3-games/ela-games/adjectives.html
This website has some fun adjective games that you can play.

About the Author

Darice Bailer has written many books for children. She has wanted to be a writer ever since she was in elementary school.